# Transpersonal Psychology

Chloe Martin

Chloe Martin

## Copyright Page

Chloe Martin

# Index

# What is Transpersonal Psychology

Transpersonal psychology is a branch of psychology that seeks to go beyond the traditional study of the mind and human behavior. It is not content with explaining how we think, feel, or act from a clinical or behavioral perspective. It goes much further. Transpersonal psychology focuses on the deep, spiritual, and transcendent aspects of the human experience. Its purpose is not simply to alleviate suffering or cure disorders, but to expand consciousness and help humans remember who they truly are, beyond their name, their history, or their personality. It is an invitation to look within oneself, to connect with what is most essential, with the soul, and from there live a life of meaning and purpose.

This branch of psychology emerged in the second half of the 20th century, when several psychologists and psychiatrists began to feel that classical approaches were insufficient to explain certain profound human experiences: mystical states, moments of ecstasy, experiences of unity with the universe, spiritual awakenings, or even near-death experiences. These phenomena did not fit into traditional analytical frameworks. Thus, figures such as Abraham Maslow, Stanislav Grof, and Ken Wilber, among others, began to develop a psychology that integrated body, mind, soul, and spirit, recognizing that all these levels are real and inseparable parts of the human being.

Unlike conventional psychology, which often focuses on problems, symptoms, or traumas, transpersonal psychology also works with human potential. It is interested in what we can become when we transcend the limitations of the ego. It invites us to look beyond our limiting beliefs, our emotional wounds, and even beyond the identity we have constructed throughout our lives. It seeks to lead us to a higher state of consciousness, where we stop identifying exclusively with the personal self and begin to recognize a broader, deeper, and more luminous identity.

The word “transpersonal” literally means “beyond the personal.” This doesn't imply rejecting or ignoring our individual history, but rather transcending it—integrating it into a deeper level of consciousness. Imagine your personality as a wave in the ocean. It has shape, direction, and unique characteristics. But in essence, it's no different from the ocean. Transpersonal psychology seeks to help you remember that you are not just the wave, but also the ocean. This expansion of consciousness profoundly changes the way we live, relate to others, make decisions, and face difficulties.

One of the great contributions of this approach is that it recognizes the value of spiritual practices in the therapeutic process. Meditation, contemplation, conscious breathing, expanded states of consciousness, and other tools previously considered outside the realm of science are seriously and rigorously integrated into the processes of self-knowledge and healing. Transpersonal psychology is not tied to a particular religion, but it does recognize that the spiritual is a legitimate dimension of human experience, as important as the emotional, cognitive, or biological.

In this sense, this type of psychology isn't satisfied with just making a person function better in their daily life. It aims for something deeper: for the person to awaken. Awakening, in transpersonal terms, means realizing that we are much more than what we thought we were. That there is within us a source of wisdom, peace, and love that depends on nothing external. And when we connect with that source, when we recognize and cultivate it, we begin to live from a different place. Life takes on new meaning. Everything makes sense. And then we stop chasing happiness outside, only to discover that it was always within.

This awakening isn't something that happens overnight. It's a process. Sometimes slow, sometimes accelerated. An inward journey that involves looking at our shadows, facing our fears, letting go of old beliefs, and opening ourselves to a greater truth. Transpersonal psychology accompanies us on this journey. It doesn't tell us what to believe, but invites us to explore. It doesn't give us absolute answers, but it teaches us to ask deeper questions. And, above all, it reminds us that human beings have immense, sacred potential, which cannot be reduced to a formula or a diagnosis.

When a person begins to live from a transpersonal consciousness, their life changes. They begin to see more clearly, feel more deeply, and listen more attentively. They become more compassionate, freer, and more authentic. They learn to be present, to value the simple, to be grateful for what they previously took for granted. They connect with life, with others, with their own essential being. And this transforms their inner world, but also their outer world.

Ultimately, transpersonal psychology is an invitation to remember. To remember who we are in essence: pure consciousness, love, presence. To remember that there is something greater than ourselves, but that also dwells within us. And to live from that memory, not as a theory, but as a living and ongoing experience. It is a path that calls us to look within, to heal, to awaken, and to live fully, with an open soul and a burning heart.

# The Map of Human Consciousness

Talking about the map of human consciousness is like talking about a journey. But not an outward journey, but an inward one. A profound journey that goes from the lowest levels of perception and understanding to elevated states of clarity, love, and wisdom. Consciousness is not something static. It is not a switch that is either on or off. It is a spectrum, a scale, a series of steps we can climb with inner work, meaningful experiences, and a willingness to transform. Just as the body can develop and strengthen with exercise, consciousness can also grow, expand, and awaken.

The idea of a map of consciousness isn't just a pretty metaphor. It's a concrete tool that allows us to understand what level we're at and where we can go next. One of the best-known maps is the one proposed by David R. Hawkins, a psychiatrist and spiritual teacher who dedicated much of his life to investigating how different emotional and mental states correspond to different levels of consciousness. His map ranges from the densest states, such as shame or guilt, to the highest, such as peace and enlightenment. Each level has its own vibration, its way of seeing the world, its own particular energy. And the most interesting thing is that we've all, at some point, passed through several of these levels.

At the lowest levels of consciousness, life is perceived as a constant struggle. Shame, for example, is one of the most painful states of being. At that level, the person feels broken, inadequate, and unworthy. It's not just that they believe they've done something wrong; they feel that they themselves are wrong. A little higher is guilt, where there is still pain, but some awareness of responsibility already appears. Then there is apathy, where hope is lost. The person feels that nothing makes sense, that nothing matters. It's a feeling of total emptiness. These levels are dark, heavy, and many people live in them without even knowing that there is another way to experience reality.

As we move up the map, the energy shifts. Instead of rejection, anger begins to emerge. Although it may seem negative, anger has a power that the previous levels lack. It's a drive to action, a signal that something isn't right and needs to change. Higher up is pride, which now feels like an accomplishment compared to guilt or apathy. But pride still relies on ego, on comparing oneself to others, on feeling superior. At this level, consciousness is still fragile, although more stable.

Then we reach a turning point: courage. At this level, life is no longer seen as something to be endured, but as something to be faced. The person begins to take responsibility for their existence. They no longer see themselves as victims, but as creators of their experience. From here, everything changes. States such as neutrality, willingness, acceptance, and reason emerge. The person begins to live with more balance, more openness, and more mental clarity. They no longer react so much from emotion, but from a deeper understanding.

But the journey doesn't end there. Beyond reason, which is the highest level of the logical mind, lie the truly transpersonal levels. Deep acceptance, unconditional love, the joy of being, inner peace. In these states, the person no longer lives from the ego. They connect with their essence, with others, and with the universe in a much more harmonious way. They stop seeing separation and begin to experience unity. There is no longer struggle. There is surrender, trust, gratitude. And at the highest levels, even beyond peace, lies enlightenment. Not as an unattainable goal, but as a pure state of consciousness, free of duality, where there is no longer a "self" that separates itself from the rest.

This map isn't just theory. It has immense practical uses. It allows us to recognize what emotional and mental state we find ourselves in most of the time. It gives us clues. For example, if you live in constant complaint, if everything bothers you, if you feel like the world is against you, you're probably at a level of consciousness where victimization or anger predominates. If you feel a strong need to be right, to control everything, you may be at the level of pride. And if, on the other hand, you feel peace even when things don't go as expected, if you trust in life, if you can see beauty even in chaos, then you're vibrating at higher levels.

Consciousness is dynamic. It changes. It's not about pigeonholing yourself into one level and staying there. We can have moments of deep connection and then fall back into old patterns. That's part of the process. The important thing is to know that the map exists, that there is a path, and that every step we take toward higher consciousness transforms not only our lives, but also the lives of those around us. Because consciousness is contagious. An awakened heart has the power to awaken others.

Understanding this map also gives us compassion. It helps us understand that a person who acts with hatred, envy, or aggression isn't fundamentally "bad," but rather is living from a lower level of consciousness. They haven't yet seen what they can be. And this understanding doesn't excuse, but it does soften the judgment. It allows us to see others as travelers on the same path, each at their own pace, with their own challenges. And the same applies to us. We don't need to blame ourselves for being at a low level. We just need to acknowledge it and begin to rise.

Each level we ascend on the map of consciousness allows us to see more, feel more, and live better. Not because everything is perfect, but because our way of relating to life changes. From guilt or anger, any problem seems like a monster. From love or peace, that same problem can become an opportunity for growth. That's how powerful consciousness is. That's how profound this journey is.

Knowing the map is the first step. The next is using it. Observe ourselves honestly, without judgment, and ask ourselves: From what level am I living? Where do I spend most of my time? What level would I like to reach? What thoughts, emotions, or attitudes do I need to leave behind to continue rising? The answers don't always come immediately, but the search itself elevates us. Because whoever dares to look within is already walking toward the light. And that path, although challenging, is also the most beautiful we can travel.

# The Ego

Talking about the ego is like talking about a character we all carry within us and that, without realizing it, directs many of our decisions, reactions, and thoughts. The ego is not an enemy, nor something we need to eliminate, but it is something we need to deeply understand if we want to grow in consciousness and live more authentically. The ego is that part of us that is built on our beliefs, our past experiences, what we were told we were, what we learned to do to feel accepted or valued. It's like a mask we put on to navigate the world, but it doesn't represent all of who we are.

From the time we are children, we begin to form an idea of who we are. We are told our names, given labels, compared to others, rewarded for certain behaviors and punished for others. Little by little, we create an identity: "I am smart," "I am clumsy," "I am nice," "I am insecure," "I am strong," "I am weak." This identity is what we call ego. It's not a bad thing. In fact, at many moments in our lives, the ego protects us, helps us survive, and organizes us mentally. The problem arises when we believe that's all we are. When we identify completely with the character and forget that there is something much bigger and truer within us.

The ego thrives on comparisons. It's always measuring, evaluating, seeking to win, to be right, to stand out, or to defend itself. It's afraid of looking bad, it struggles to accept its mistakes, and it's uncomfortable with uncertainty. It has a constant need for control and validation. It wants to be recognized, admired, and accepted. Therefore, we often act not from what we truly feel or desire, but from what we believe will make us look better to others. We live trying to maintain an image, a façade, and this wears us down profoundly.

One of the ego's strongest functions is to protect us from pain. When we've experienced emotional wounds, rejections, or failures, the ego builds defenses so we don't suffer again. But those same defenses that were once useful become prisons over time. For example, if someone was heavily criticized as a child, they may have developed a perfectionist ego to avoid judgment. That person will live obsessed with doing everything right, but inside, they will be filled with a fear of making mistakes. Another person, if they were ignored or undervalued, may develop a narcissistic ego, exaggerating their worth so others won't notice their insecurity. Thus, the ego distances us from our essence, from our authentic selves, to keep us safe, even if that means living with anxiety, rigidity, or disconnection.

The ego can't stand feeling vulnerable. It struggles to accept that it doesn't know, that it needs help, that it's afraid. Because of this, it often acts arrogantly, harshly, or with indifference. But deep down, every ego hides a wound. A part of us that wasn't heard, that wasn't loved as it needed, and that still seeks to be seen. And that's the key: the ego mustn't be destroyed, it must be understood. It's not about rejecting the ego, but about illuminating it. About looking at it with compassion and saying: thank you for protecting me, but now I want to live from a different place. I want to truly know myself.

As we advance on our path of consciousness, we begin to notice when we are acting from the ego and when we are acting from the soul. The ego wants to have, accumulate, control. The soul wants to be, share, flow. The ego reacts with fear, anger, and defense. The soul responds with peace, presence, and openness. The ego seeks validation from outside. The soul already knows it is valuable. This contrast becomes increasingly clear when we observe ourselves honestly. It's not about eliminating the ego, but rather about not letting it control us. We can use it when necessary, but not live trapped in it.

A clear sign that we are dominated by the ego is when we live from a constant need for approval. If a negative comment destroys us, if we can't tolerate criticism, if we feel worthless when someone doesn't look at us or compliment us, then we are overly identified with the image the ego has constructed. This generates suffering because it places our value in the hands of others. And the most dangerous thing is that, in this state, it is never enough. Something is always missing. We always feel we should be more, have more, achieve more. We live in a constant state of lack.

Another way the ego operates is through judgment. We judge others to make ourselves feel better. We judge our emotions, our past decisions, our failures. The ego doesn't accept imperfection because it believes that if something is wrong with us, then we are unworthy. But higher consciousness recognizes that being human is being imperfect, and that precisely in that imperfection lies beauty, humility, and the possibility of evolution. When we stop judging ourselves, when we let go of the need to be perfect, the soul begins to speak louder.

It's also important to understand that the ego doesn't disappear overnight. It's part of the human structure. Even people with very high levels of consciousness still have egos. The difference is that they no longer identify with them. They observe them, acknowledge them, and choose not to follow their impulses. That's a great freedom: to be able to see the ego without being led by it. To be able to notice when it wants to react and, instead of acting automatically, to stop, breathe, and connect with what's essential. That's where true transformation begins.

A powerful practice for deactivating the ego is self-observation. Begin to notice, without judgment, when I'm acting to please, when I want to be right, when I feel superior or inferior. Each time I notice these internal movements, I have the opportunity to choose something else. Choose humility, empathy, silence. Another practice is gratitude. The ego always focuses on what's missing. The soul is grateful for what is there. Being grateful for the simple, the everyday, what we take for granted, connects us to a deeper, more loving consciousness.

Finally, we must know that the ego is not the enemy of spirituality, but it can be an obstacle if we don't recognize it. It's like a voice that always wants to be in control of the steering wheel, but if we learn to listen to it without obeying it, it loses its power. True growth begins when we stop reacting to that voice and begin to live from a broader presence. A presence that doesn't need to prove anything, that doesn't compete, that doesn't compare. It just is. And that presence, when expressed, brings peace, authenticity, and freedom. Then, we no longer live to maintain an image, but to be true to our truth. And in that truth, the ego gently dissolves, like a mist at dawn.

# The Power of Attention and Presence

Attention and presence are two of the most profound powers we have as human beings, yet we often overlook them. We live in a fast-paced world, full of stimuli, distractions, and demands. Our minds jump from one thought to another like a restless monkey. We're physically in one place, but mentally in another. We think about what happened yesterday, what might happen tomorrow, what we didn't do, what we should have said. And meanwhile, life slips away. The present moment, which is the only thing that truly exists, is lost in the noise of our minds. That's where the power of attention and presence comes in: as a gateway back to the now, to the only moment where we can truly live, feel, and transform.

Being present isn't simply being there physically. It's being there with our whole being. With our senses awake, our mind attentive, our heart open. Presence is a quality of awareness in which we don't just see, but truly observe. We don't just listen, but truly hear. We don't just touch, but we feel deeply. It's as if everything becomes more real, more vivid, more alive. Because when we are present, everything takes on a special intensity. Even the most mundane things are transformed. Drinking a glass of water, looking at the sky, feeling the air on our skin. Life ceases to be something that passes without our noticing and becomes a rich, intimate, and meaningful experience.

Attention, for its part, is the tool that allows us to enter that presence. It's like the focus of a flashlight that we can direct at will. Wherever we place our attention, there goes our energy. If we place our attention on fear, that fear grows. If we place our attention on gratitude, gratitude expands. Most people don't manage their attention. It's hijacked by automatic thoughts, by mental habits, by the constant bombardment of external information. But when we begin to train our attention, we discover that we can regain control of our minds and our lives.

A simple and powerful practice is observing your breath. Bringing your attention to the air entering and leaving your body. Without trying to change it, just feeling it. At first, it may seem boring or difficult because your mind wants to wander elsewhere. But if we persevere, something begins to happen. We calm down. We center ourselves. We begin to experience moments of true inner silence. It's not an empty silence, but one filled with presence. It's in that space that we begin to clearly see what was previously hidden by mental noise.

The power of attention is also revealed in relationships. Being truly present with someone is an act of profound love. It's not just about hearing what they say, but being with them completely, without thinking about how we'll respond, without judging, without interrupting. Most people aren't used to being truly listened to. And when someone does this, they feel seen, valued, understood. Presence has the power to heal, to connect, to transform bonds. It's a silent way of saying to the other: I am here with you, completely, without distractions.

Furthermore, when we live from awareness and presence, we begin to break free from autopilot. We stop reacting on impulse and begin responding with awareness. We observe our thoughts before believing them. We feel our emotions before acting on them. That pause between stimulus and response is where true change occurs. We are no longer slaves to old patterns, but creators of new ways of being. Presence gives us the inner space we need to choose from the soul, not from habit.

Attention also has a magical quality: what we observe clearly enough begins to transform. If we bring loving attention to an emotional wound, that wound begins to heal. If we bring attention to a tension in the body, that tension begins to loosen. If we bring attention to our repetitive thoughts, they lose their power over us. Attention acts like a light that reveals, but also like a warmth that softens. We don't need to make great efforts. Just look sincerely. Just be there, present with what is, without wanting to change it immediately.

One of the most common obstacles to living in presence is the belief that we don't have time. But the truth is, you don't need time to be present. You just need intention. We can practice presence while washing dishes, while walking down the street, while talking to someone. It's not about adding another task to the list. It's about doing what we already do, but with greater awareness. Being where we are, fully. Feeling what we feel, without escaping. Seeing what we see, without distraction. Thus, life becomes richer, more real, more true.

Another obstacle is judgment. When we try to be present, thoughts often arise like, "I'm not doing it right," "this isn't working," "my mind won't shut up." But that's also part of the process. Presence doesn't require perfection. It only demands gentle, continuous attention, without struggle. Accepting what happens without trying to force it. Returning again and again to the now, like someone returning home. It doesn't matter how many times you get distracted. What matters is that you return. That return is the muscle that strengthens your awareness.

Living in mindfulness and presence doesn't mean disconnecting from the world or not planning. It means living more deeply, more connectedly, with more meaning. It means being so present that we begin to perceive life not as a series of tasks to be completed, but as an experience that unfolds moment by moment. Every moment becomes an opportunity to awaken. We don't need everything to be perfect. We just need to be there, open, available. Because in that state, any situation, no matter how difficult, can become a teacher. And any moment, no matter how simple, can fill us with light.

The greatest gift we can give ourselves and others is presence. In a world that runs, demands, and pressures, presence is a silent revolution. It's the art of returning to the essential. And the essential isn't somewhere else, isn't at another time. It's here. Now. In this instant. In this breath. In this heartbeat. That's the power of attention. That's the miracle of presence. When we learn to live from this, our whole life becomes sacred. Because we stop looking for something outside of ourselves and begin to find everything within.

# The Psychological Shadow and its Integration

There's a part of us we often prefer not to look at, a hidden area we avoid because it makes us uncomfortable or scares us. That part is what psychology calls the shadow. It's not an esoteric or mystical concept. It's simply everything we've repressed, denied, or hidden from ourselves.

These are thoughts, emotions, impulses, and aspects of our personality that don't fit with the image we want to have of ourselves or with what we were taught was acceptable. The psychological shadow is a natural part of being human. We all have it. And the most interesting thing is that the more we deny it, the more power it has over our lives.

From the time we're little, we learn what's "good" and what's "bad" according to our family, culture, or religion. We're told to be calm, kind, responsible, and polite. And then, when we feel anger, envy, fear, or desires that don't fit that ideal image, we begin to hide them. Not because we're fake, but because we need to feel accepted. This is how the shadow is born. Everything that doesn't fit the image we want to present, we tuck away in a deep corner of our minds. But it doesn't go away. It just hides.

The shadow manifests itself in many ways. Sometimes, in intense emotions we can't control. Other times, in exaggerated reactions to certain people or situations. Something inside is triggered, and we don't quite understand why. For example, if someone really annoys us for no apparent reason, it's possible that person is reflecting a part of us we don't want to see. Maybe it's their ego, their arrogance, their way of expressing themselves. But if they annoy us so intensely, they're probably tapping into a part of our shadow. In psychology, this is called projection: we attribute to others what we don't accept in ourselves.

Another way the shadow appears is in our contradictions. We say we're patient, but we explode easily. We think we're generous, but we feel jealous when someone else succeeds. We think we're compassionate, but we judge those who are different. These contradictions don't mean we're bad or hypocritical. They only indicate that there are internal aspects we haven't integrated. And that's precisely the key: integration doesn't mean justifying or acting from the shadow, but rather recognizing it, accepting it, and learning to live with it consciously.

Shadow integration is one of the most important processes on the path to consciousness. Because true inner transformation cannot be achieved if we continue to divide ourselves internally, if we continue to fight against parts of ourselves. The goal is not to eliminate the "bad" and keep only the "good," but to become whole. To be whole humans, capable of recognizing both our light and our darkness. In fact, many of our talents and gifts are hidden behind the shadow. Sometimes we repress strength, creativity, or sensuality because we were led to believe they were dangerous or inappropriate. But by integrating the shadow, we recover all of that.

A fundamental tool in this work is nonjudgmental self-observation. Begin to notice our reactions with curiosity rather than criticism. Ask yourself: Why does this bother me so much? What part of me am I trying to hide? What do I not want to admit? It's not about blaming yourself or feeling bad, but rather about observing honestly. It's also helpful to pay attention to dreams, as the shadow often appears in them with symbols or characters that make us uncomfortable. The unconscious tries to communicate, to show what we have hidden.

It's important to understand that the shadow isn't just the "negative." We can also repress positive qualities if we ever feel they are dangerous or causing us problems. For example, a very intelligent person who was ridiculed for excelling in school may hide their ability to avoid attention. Or someone who was judged for being very sensitive may harden themselves and act as if nothing affects them. These are also forms of shadow. And by integrating them, we recover essential parts of our soul.

Integrating the shadow is an act of courage. It requires looking inward with sincerity, accepting what we find without disguising it, and opening ourselves to a more complete vision of ourselves. It's not always comfortable, but it is profoundly liberating. Because until we do, we will continue to be governed by those hidden parts. We will make decisions based on fear, rejection, the need for approval, or suppressed anger. But when we begin to understand our shadow, we stop being puppets of our unconscious emotions. We begin to choose with more clarity, with more presence, with more freedom.

There's a great paradox in this process: the more we resist our shadow, the stronger it becomes. But when we look at it head-on, without fear, without judgment, it begins to lose its power. Like a monster that seemed gigantic in the darkness, but when we turn on the light, we see it wasn't so big. By integrating it, we stop fighting against ourselves. And that gives us immense peace. Because we no longer have to pretend, we no longer need to maintain an image. We can be real. Human. Imperfect, yes, but whole.

A practical way to begin this work is to write. Take a notebook and write down with complete honesty what we feel, what we think, what we're ashamed to admit. Without filters. Without trying to be correct. Just letting out what's inside. Another way is through internal dialogue: talking to our shadow, asking it what it needs, what it wants to tell us, why it acts the way it does. This practice may seem strange at first, but it's deeply revealing. Because everything we've denied still has a voice, and if we don't listen to it, it expresses itself in other ways: with anxiety, with illness, with conflict.

Shadow integration isn't a final destination, but rather a continuous journey. There will always be deeper layers, new revelations. But every step we take in that direction makes us more authentic, more aware, more free. We learn to embrace our contradictions, to live without masks, to relate to others from a more genuine place. We no longer need to defend ourselves so much or hide. Because we know who we are. With our lights and our shadows. And from that integrity, we can live with more compassion, more strength, and more truth.

Ultimately, the shadow is not the enemy of the light. It is part of it. It is like the night that allows us to cherish the day. Like winter that prepares for spring. Only when we dare to look at the darkness within us can we discover the true depth of our light. Because that light is not something superficial or decorative. It is the capacity to love even what we don't understand, to accept even what is difficult for us, to heal even what we thought was lost. And that capacity, once awakened, becomes the most powerful guide on our path of transformation.

# Pain as a Portal of Transformation

Pain is one of those human experiences we all share, although each of us experiences it differently. There are many types of pain: physical, emotional, psychological, spiritual. Some hurt briefly, and others stay with us for years. Some we understand, others baffle us. Some pain comes from loss, rejection, betrayal, illness, or simply from the inner emptiness we sometimes feel without knowing why. What is common to all of us is that we don't like to feel pain. We will do almost anything to avoid it, distract ourselves from it, or eliminate it as quickly as possible. But pain, when we look at it through different eyes, can become a profound portal to transformation.

Most of us have been raised to fear pain. We were taught that it's an enemy, that it must be silenced or covered up with something: with medicine, with work, with entertainment, with food, with relationships. And it's not wrong to seek relief; it's part of the survival instinct. But when we become experts at avoiding pain, we also become experts at disconnecting from ourselves. Because pain doesn't appear to punish us; it appears to show us something. It's a signal, a messenger. And if instead of running away from it, we learn to listen to it, it can reveal very deep parts of our soul.

Pain has the ability to shatter the structures we took for granted. A breakup, for example, can unravel an entire identity we had built around another person. The death of a loved one can call into question everything we believed about life and death. An existential crisis can shake our certainties, our plans, our sense of purpose. And yes, at first, that hurts. It hurts because we're losing something. But it also hurts because something inside us is awakening. Pain forces us to look beyond the surface. It pushes us inward, toward questions we've never asked before. It makes us pause, stop living on automatic. And in that pause, the transformation begins.

Many people report that their darkest moments were also the beginning of their brightest journeys. Not because pain in itself is good, but because when we truly face it, when we consciously move through it, a door opens. A door to a new way of living, of feeling, of understanding ourselves. It's as if pain tears away a superficial layer of our lives and leaves us staring at what's essential. Suddenly, what seemed important is no longer so. And what we took for granted becomes sacred. We learn to value the simple, to connect with our vulnerability, to recognize the fragility of everything. And that makes us more human, more compassionate, wiser.

The process of transformation through grief is neither linear nor rapid. There are moments of clarity and others of confusion. There are breakthroughs and setbacks. Sometimes we think we've healed, and suddenly the pain returns with a vengeance. That doesn't mean we're failing; it means we're going deeper. Because grief has layers. And every time we touch one, the possibility of seeing deeper opens up. The important thing isn't to avoid those waves, but to learn to sustain ourselves within them. To know that pain doesn't destroy us, that we can move through it and emerge more whole on the other side.

A key part of the journey is allowing ourselves to feel. We've often repressed our emotions so much that when pain appears, we don't know what to do with it. We tell ourselves things like, "I have to be strong," "this shouldn't affect me so much," "I don't have time to feel this way." But being strong doesn't mean denying what we feel. Being strong is having the courage to feel everything. To cry when we need to cry, to scream when necessary, to remain silent when there are no words. Pain wants to be felt, not analyzed or immediately resolved. And when we give it space, it transforms itself.

It's also important to stop comparing ourselves. Each person's journey is unique. What may be a mild blow to one person may be a deep wound to another. And what one person resolves in weeks may take years for another. There's no rule. Pain isn't measured in time or intensity. It's measured in honesty. Are we willing to face it? Are we willing to let it transform us? Because what's at stake isn't how much we suffer, but how much we allow ourselves to be touched by the experience. How much we allow it to change us from within.

Another key is opening ourselves to support. We often believe we have to go through pain alone, that no one would understand us, or that we would be a burden to others. But shared pain is lessened. Not because the other person resolves it for us, but because we feel seen, supported, and acknowledged. And that, too, is healing. Talking, writing, and seeking professional or spiritual help is not a sign of weakness, but of self-love. Because asking for support is also a way of honoring what we are experiencing.

At the heart of pain is a seed of wisdom. A part of us knows, even if it's deep down, that this difficult time has meaning. That it's not in vain. That something is being purified, cleansed, reorganized. It's like when a forest burns and at first it seems all is lost, but over time, the earth is renewed and new, stronger shoots appear. This is what happens in the soul. Pain can be that fire that burns away the old to allow the new to be born. And although we don't always immediately see the meaning, over time, we often understand why it was necessary.

The transformation that comes from pain isn't just personal. When someone has gone through their own hell and emerged with a more open heart, they become a beacon for others. Because their presence conveys something profound. They don't need to say much, just be there. And that is already medicine. Pain, when worked with awareness, becomes a source of gentle power, of true humility, of sincere compassion. Because those who have experienced pain firsthand no longer judge so quickly, no longer speak from a theoretical perspective, no longer live from a superficial perspective.

Accepting pain as part of the journey doesn't mean resigning or letting yourself be crushed. It means trusting that everything has a process, even the hardest things. It means walking with patience, with tenderness toward oneself, with respect for one's inner time. And it also means being willing to see that sometimes the greatest blessings come disguised as crises. That sometimes you have to hit rock bottom in order to push yourself upward with greater strength. That the soul has its own methods of awakening, and pain is one of them.

So, instead of rejecting pain, we can begin to ask ourselves what it's trying to teach us. We can learn to listen to it like someone who listens to a wise man who doesn't speak with sweet words, but with a profound truth. Because behind every tear lies a seed of transformation. Behind every emptiness lies a possibility of rebirth. And behind every painful experience, there is a door. A door that only opens when we stop resisting it and begin to walk inward, with an open heart and the confidence that, even if it hurts, we are moving toward our deepest truth.

# Non-Ordinary States of Consciousness

Human consciousness is not a single, fixed, and static entity. It is a broad and flexible field that can expand, contract, deepen, or elevate depending on many factors. Most people live their daily lives in what is known as the ordinary state of consciousness, that is, a way of perceiving reality focused on the external, the mundane, the logical, and the immediate. In this state, we go to work, solve problems, talk to others, and fulfill our responsibilities. But this is not the only way the human mind can operate. There are other, deeper, broader, and richer states that we call non-ordinary states of consciousness. These states allow us to access hidden parts of our being, understand life from a different perspective, and connect with more spiritual or subtle dimensions of existence.

A non-ordinary state of consciousness isn't simply being distracted or daydreaming. Nor is it being randomly under the influence of drugs. It's a form of perception in which our awareness moves away from habitual logic, from the sense of limited self, and opens to a more intuitive, more symbolic, more connected experience with the whole. There are many ways to enter these states, and many reasons why someone might seek them: deep emotional healing, spiritual connection, consciousness exploration, trauma insight, inner expansion, creativity, or simply the need to feel something beyond the known.

One of the most common paths to accessing non-ordinary states of consciousness is through contemplative practices such as deep meditation. When we meditate for long periods and with sustained attention, the mind begins to calm, thoughts slow down, and we begin to perceive things that we simply ignore in the ordinary state. We can feel a connection with everything around us, experience a sense of unity, of causeless peace, of pure presence. These states cannot be fully described in words because they do not belong to ordinary language. They are experiential experiences, where one "knows" something without needing to explain it. It is as if the soul remembers something the mind had forgotten.

Another powerful path is conscious breathing, such as holotropic breathwork. This technique, developed by psychiatrist Stanislav Grof, uses intense breathing patterns along with evocative music to induce deep states of consciousness. During these sessions, people may relive old memories, experience repressed emotions, experience symbolic visions, or come into contact with a spiritual dimension. It is an intense process, not always comfortable, but profoundly transformative. Here, the body and psyche are freed from blockages, and the person can undergo processes of catharsis, understanding, or emotional release without the need for speech.

There are also states induced by art, dance, singing, or deep contemplation of nature. When someone enters a kind of creative trance, they lose track of time, merge with the activity, and something beyond their ego seems to take control. They don't think; they simply are. They are present, flowing, in a state of connection that transcends logic. This is very common in musicians, painters, and writers, but also in people who walk through the forest mindfully, or who silently observe the sea and suddenly feel that everything makes sense. These are brief moments, perhaps, but very revealing.

We must also mention the non-ordinary states induced by sacred plants, used for centuries by indigenous cultures in ceremonial contexts. These plants, such as ayahuasca, peyote, or psilocybin mushrooms, are not simply hallucinogenic substances. They are powerful tools that, when used with respect, proper guidance, and in a spiritual context, can open doors to very deep dimensions of the being. People who have had experiences with these medicines report clear visions, encounters with archetypes, intense emotional experiences, contact with their own fears, and in many cases, a feeling of unconditional love or unity with the universe. However, they are not an easy path, nor should they be used as entertainment. They require preparation, restraint, and above all, a clear intention.

Lucid dreams are also part of non-ordinary states of consciousness. To dream lucidly is to know that we are dreaming while we are within the dream. In that moment, the dreamer can interact with the dream content, explore their inner world, ask for guidance, face fears, heal traumas, or simply experience a freedom that is not possible in everyday life. Lucid dreams can be trained with practice and are a fascinating gateway to the unconscious. In fact, many ancient cultures considered dreams a bridge between this world and other planes of existence. And when we experience them lucidly, we understand why.

The most important thing when talking about these non-ordinary states is not to romanticize or idealize them, but to understand that they are tools. They are not the ultimate goal, but rather a path to deeper self-knowledge, healing, or spiritual expansion. What one discovers in these states must be integrated into daily life, because there's no point in having a mystical experience if the next day we continue to react from the ego, repeating old patterns, fleeing from the present. True transformation is not what happens during the expanded state, but what we do with it afterward.

Furthermore, it's important to understand that these states aren't appropriate for everyone at all times. Some people may feel overwhelmed, confused, or even scared if they enter them unprepared. Therefore, it's always best to be accompanied by someone with experience, to be well-informed, and above all, to listen to yourself. Consciousness knows what it needs, and forcing an experience out of curiosity can end up distancing us from ourselves instead of bringing us closer.

The beauty of this topic is that you don't need a wealth of experience to begin exploring. All you need to do is observe yourself more deeply, open spaces of silence, breathe more attentively, write down what you feel, and gaze at the sky without rushing. We all have access to these states, not as something exotic, but as part of our nature. Human consciousness is like an ocean, and most of us only know the shore. But if we dare to dive in, to explore, to trust that inner calling, we can discover immense landscapes within ourselves. Places where there is no judgment, where everything feels connected, where even the most painful things can find meaning.

Non-ordinary states of consciousness remind us that we are more than a name, a body, or a personal story. They invite us to let go for a moment of the identity we think we are, to discover who we truly are: pure consciousness, a living presence, part of a larger whole that we are only beginning to understand. And although these experiences may seem distant or strange, the truth is that they are closer than we imagine. They require only one thing: a willingness to look inward with openness, with respect, and with the certainty that within us lies a universe waiting to be discovered.

# The Soul

To speak of the soul is to enter a profound, mysterious, and at the same time very intimate territory. Although we cannot see it with our eyes or touch it with our hands, we have all felt its presence at some point. It is that part of us that seems ageless, that does not change with the passing of the years, that silently observes behind everything we do. It is not the mind that thinks, nor the body that feels, nor the emotions that come and go. The soul is that which remains when everything else moves. It is who we are at our most essential.

Since ancient times, all cultures have spoken of the soul in different ways. Some called it spirit, others essence, others divine spark. But they all agreed on one thing: within each human being there is something greater than identity, something eternal, something sacred. Transpersonal Psychology takes up this idea, not from a religious perspective, but from lived experience. It invites us to recognize that, beyond our thoughts, behaviors, or traumas, there is a deeper dimension that deserves to be heard and cultivated. That dimension is the soul.

The soul can't be explained, it can be felt. It isn't fully understood through logic, but it is recognized through experience. There are moments in life when the soul emerges powerfully. It may be when we look at a sunset and feel like time has stopped. It may be when we hear a song that gives us goosebumps for no apparent reason. It may be when we hug someone and experience a connection that goes beyond words. It may also appear in the midst of pain, when everything falls apart, and yet something within us remains standing, silent, as if it knows that everything is okay even though our minds tell us otherwise.

Living in touch with the soul doesn't mean ignoring reality or floating in a fantasy world. On the contrary. It means living with more depth, with more meaning, with more presence. It means looking at life as if every moment had a sacred value, as if everything that happens to us were full of messages to awaken us. The soul isn't in the sky; it's right here, in the everyday, in the simple, in the true. But to listen to it, you have to learn to be silent. You have to lower the noise of your mind, stop, look inward, and be willing to feel.

The soul speaks a different language than the ego. While the ego seeks recognition, control, and security, the soul seeks truth, growth, and connection. The soul is in no hurry, because it knows the deepest moments of existence. It is not interested in external perfection, but in authenticity. Sometimes the soul leads us down paths we don't understand, but which, over time, reveal their meaning. It pushes us to let go of what no longer serves us, to face what we avoid, to follow what truly moves us, even if it isn't the easiest or most logical thing to do.

One of the clearest signs that we are in touch with our soul is a feeling of fulfillment. Not a superficial happiness, but a deep peace, an inner "yes" that needs no explanation. It's as if everything falls into place, as if we are where we were meant to be. This feeling can appear in the midst of a job we love, in a deep conversation, in a shared laugh with a loved one, or even in solitude, when we feel we need nothing else to be well. The soul doesn't need external things to feel alive. It's enough to be in coherence with who we truly are.

But we don't always live from the soul. We often disconnect. We lose ourselves in the constant doing, in the demands, in the masks we use to fit in or to protect ourselves. And when that happens, we begin to feel a void. A tiredness that can't be erased with physical rest. A lack of meaning that neither success nor consumption can fill. That emptiness is the sign that we've lost touch with our soul. It's not a punishment, it's a calling. It's the soul's way of telling us: come back to yourself, remember who you are, stop running.

Reconnecting with the soul doesn't require grand rituals or distant journeys. Sometimes it's enough to stop. Breathe. Ask ourselves honestly: Is what I'm doing true to me? Is what I'm feeling what my soul needs or what others expect? Am I being loyal to my truth or am I just surviving? The answers aren't always easy, but they are the beginning of the journey. Honesty with oneself is the door that opens contact with the soul. Because the soul cannot inhabit a persona. It only reveals itself when we are genuine.

It also helps a lot to return to the basics. Spending time in nature, writing, meditating, creating, being in silence, listening to uplifting music. Anything that makes us feel more alive, more whole, more present is food for the soul. And when the soul is nourished, it shows. We feel more at peace, lighter, more connected to everything. We no longer need to have everything figured out or know what's going to happen next. It's enough to be here, to trust that life guides us from within.

Along the path of personal and spiritual development, there comes a time when it's no longer about accumulating more knowledge, but about deepening the experience. Going slower, but deeper. And that's where the soul becomes our most trusted guide. It doesn't need degrees, certifications, or external approval. It just needs us to be willing to listen. Because the soul always speaks, even when we don't hear it. It's there, patiently waiting for us to come home.

Listening to the soul can bring about change. It may mean leaving a job that no longer represents us, ending a relationship that limits us, starting a project that scares us, moving to a new city, letting go of old ideas. It's not always comfortable. But it's always true. Because the soul never leads us where we shouldn't go. Its guidance isn't that of a whim or a passing desire. It's that of a deep calling. That feeling that tells us: this is the path, even if you don't quite know where it leads. Trust.

And perhaps the most beautiful thing of all is that when we live from the soul, we inspire others to do the same. There's no need to preach or convince. Just live coherently, with love, with presence. Because the soul recognizes itself among souls. And when someone lives from that place, they become a beacon for others. Not because they have all the answers, but because they radiate a truth that can be felt. And that's what the world needs most today: people who live from their soul, who dare to be, to love, to create from their deepest essence.

The soul isn't lost, it's just hidden. And every day is an opportunity to return to it. No matter how many times we've forgotten, how many times we've fallen, how many times we've strayed. The soul is always there, waiting with infinite patience, like a flame that never goes out. We just have to stop, close our eyes, breathe deeply, and remember who we are beyond everything. Because in that memory lies freedom, fulfillment, and the true meaning of being alive.

# Intuition as an Internal Guide

Intuition is one of those human abilities that we all possess, but that we often forget, ignore, or confuse with other things. We live in a culture that has placed too much emphasis on logic, analysis, data, and the rational mind. We've been taught to make decisions from the top of our heads, to seek proof for everything, to distrust anything that can't be explained in words. However, within us exists another form of knowing. A kind of wisdom that comes not from thought or accumulated experience, but from a deeper place. That place is intuition.

Intuition is that inner voice that simply knows. It doesn't go through the process of reasoning, it doesn't need to argue or justify. It simply appears as a sudden certainty, a clear feeling, an impulse that tells us "this way" or "this way no." We've all had moments like that. Moments when we clearly felt something wasn't right, even though everything seemed to be in order. Or moments when we knew what to do without any concrete information to back it up. That's intuition speaking.

The interesting thing is that this ability isn't exclusive to special people or limited to certain situations. It's available to everyone, all the time. But for us to use it with confidence, we first need to learn to distinguish it from other inner voices that can confuse us. Because not everything we suddenly feel is intuition. Sometimes what we think is a hunch is just disguised fear, or impatient desire, or an emotional reaction. Intuition, when it's true, feels different. It has a quality of calm, of clarity, even if it's telling us something uncomfortable. It doesn't shout, it doesn't push, it doesn't despair. It whispers. And that whisper is enough to move us if we're in tune.

Intuition is intimately linked to the soul. In fact, you could say it's the language the soul uses to communicate with us. The more connected we are to our inner center, the clearer that voice becomes. But when we live from the ego, from mental noise, from fear or anxiety, intuition becomes difficult to hear. That's why it's so important to create spaces of silence, connection, and listening. It's not about performing grand rituals. Sometimes it's enough to pause for a few minutes, close our eyes, breathe deeply, and ask ourselves: How do I really feel about this? Not what I think, but what I feel deep down. The answer often comes effortlessly. It's as if something inside us already knows.

Intuition manifests itself in different ways. Sometimes it's a fleeting image that appears in the mind. Sometimes it's a physical sensation, like a knot in the stomach or an opening in the chest. Other times it's a dream, a coincidence, a phrase we hear that seems to have a direct message for us. The universe has many ways of speaking to us when we are willing to listen. The key is to trust. To trust that not everything is understood with our heads. To trust that within us there is a wiser guide than our thoughts. To trust that even if we don't have all the answers now, there is a greater intelligence that accompanies us.

One of the biggest mistakes we make is distrusting our intuition for fear of being wrong. We ask ourselves: What if I follow this guideline and it doesn't work? But there's something fundamental to understand here. Intuition doesn't guarantee that everything will be easy or perfect. What it does is show us the path that is aligned with our growth and our inner truth. Sometimes that path involves challenges, losses, or difficult decisions. But it always, absolutely always, leads us to places where we can flourish, where we can be more authentic, freer, more fulfilled.

Many people who have learned to live from their intuition report that their lives have changed radically. They no longer seek external approval for every step they take. They no longer feel lost when they have to make important decisions. They no longer need to follow other people's maps, because they have learned to trust their internal compass. This doesn't mean that everything is perfect or that there are no doubts. Intuition doesn't eliminate uncertainty, but it gives us a clear direction even in the midst of the fog. It tells us: keep walking, trust in this step, even if you can't see the destination yet.

It's important to mention that, like a muscle, intuition strengthens with use. The more we listen to it, the clearer it becomes. The more we act in line with what it tells us, the more self-confidence we gain. That's why it's so valuable to start practicing with small things. We don't have to wait for a big life decision. We can train intuition in everyday life: What do I want to eat today? Who do I want to spend this free time with? Does this place make me feel good or not? Does this conversation nourish me or drain me? Every time we make a small decision based on intuition, we give it room to grow.

We can also cultivate intuition by writing, meditating, spending time in nature, or simply being aware of what we feel in our bodies. Our body is a profound ally in this process. It often knows before our mind whether something is right for us or not. If something feels light, fluid, or calm, that's a sign. If it feels heavy, tense, or forced, that's another sign. The body doesn't lie, but we must learn to listen to it without judging or forcing it.

By developing this relationship with intuition, we begin to live with greater freedom. We no longer feel trapped by other people's opinions, mental doubts, or the need to control everything. We become more fluid, more open, more receptive. We learn to say yes when something resonates with us, even if it doesn't make sense. We learn to say no even when everyone expects us to say yes. We become more loyal to our inner truth than to external expectations. And that, in itself, is a profound act of self-love.

Ultimately, living from intuition is living in connection with our essence. It's remembering that we are more than a body and a mind. That within us dwells a loving intelligence that is always guiding our path. We just have to learn to listen to it, trust it, and follow it, step by step. We won't always know where it leads us, but if we give it space, it will take us right where we need to be. Because intuition doesn't just guide; it also protects, reveals, and transforms. And the most beautiful thing is that it has always been there, waiting for us to look at it again, to value it, to follow it with an open heart.

# Synchronicity and Signs of the Universe

There are moments in life when everything seems to mysteriously fall into place. Just when we think of someone, that person calls to us. When we feel lost, a phrase in a book, a song on the radio, or a sign on the street appears that seems to speak directly to what we carry inside. Sometimes, a conversation with a stranger leaves us with a profound lesson, or a series of events takes us, unplanned, exactly where we needed to be. These seemingly magical moments are what we call synchronicities. They are not mere coincidences. They are winks from the universe, small clues that show us that there is a larger order at work behind everything, even if we don't see it clearly.

Synchronicity was a concept developed by psychiatrist Carl Gustav Jung. He observed that many people, during their deep psychological processes, began to experience events that could not be logically explained. These weren't cause and effect, but meaningful coincidences. For example, a woman dreams of a golden scarab beetle, and the next day one flies through the window right during a therapy session. Or someone who has been feeling confused about their path for days suddenly meets someone who, unknowingly, tells them exactly what they needed to hear. Jung said that when we align ourselves with our deepest selves, the outside world begins to reflect that connection. Life becomes a mirror. And that's when synchronicities appear.

These signs are neither fantasy nor superstition. They are real in that they have an emotional, psychological, and spiritual impact on us. They make us feel that we are not alone, that there is something greater guiding us. We may not know what that "something more" is, but we feel it. It's as if life itself were speaking to us, as if there were a higher intelligence that knows exactly what we need and finds the most unexpected ways to send us a message. The curious thing is that not everyone sees these signs. Not because they don't exist, but because they aren't paying attention. To notice synchronicity, you have to be present, attentive, and sensitive. You have to learn to see things with different eyes.

In a world full of distractions, learning to read the signs of the universe becomes an act of reconnecting with what is essential. It doesn't mean that everything has a hidden meaning or that we should obsess over searching for messages everywhere. Rather, it's about developing a more intimate relationship with life. When something is repeated many times, when a symbol appears in different contexts, when we feel a special vibration when seeing, hearing, or experiencing something, we are likely facing a sign. Sometimes these signs confirm that we are on the right path. Other times, they invite us to change direction, to let go of something, to look within ourselves.

One of the most common ways the universe communicates is through repeating numbers. Many people begin to notice that they frequently see combinations like 11:11, 22:22, or 333. These numbers can appear on clocks, license plates, bills, or dates. You don't need to understand their exact meaning. Just stop, pause, and ask yourself: What was I thinking just before I saw this? What am I feeling? What decision am I about to make? Sometimes the sign is simply telling us: pay attention, you are being guided.

Another common pattern is repeated words or phrases. For example, someone mentions a country and then you see it in a movie, a song, or someone else's conversation. Or you read the same phrase in different places within a few days. These patterns aren't coincidental. They're pointing us toward an important topic, a direction to explore, a truth we must integrate. The same thing happens with animals. Some appear insistently in our lives. We dream about them, we see them in images, they physically cross our paths. Each animal has a symbolism and a message that we can explore. But beyond the traditional meaning, what's important is how it makes us feel and what it represents to us at that moment.

Synchronicity also manifests itself in encounters. People who come into our lives at just the right moment. Relationships that begin unexpectedly but bring profound learning. Souls who recognize each other just by looking at each other. These encounters are not the result of chance. They respond to an invisible dance between our inner needs and external opportunities. It's as if the universe conspires to bring together those who have something to give each other. Sometimes these relationships are lasting, other times brief but transformative. The important thing is to be open to receiving, without forcing, without controlling, without resisting.

When we begin to trust these signs, our lives change. We no longer feel that everything depends on us, on our mental effort, or on our rigid plans. We begin to collaborate with something greater. We begin to flow. We learn to let go of the need to have everything clear and perfect, and instead cultivate deep trust. We know that if we are attentive and aligned with our truth, life will show us the way step by step. This way of living is not passive. It's not about waiting for the universe to do everything. It's about acting in coherence with our intuitions while at the same time being open to what life offers us.

To cultivate this sensitivity to synchronicities and signs, it's helpful to keep a journal. Write down what we notice, the coincidences we experience, the dreams we remember, the phrases that impact us. Over time, this journal becomes a mirror of our inner process. It helps us see patterns, connect ideas, and validate experiences that, in another context, we might have dismissed as irrelevant. It's also helpful to practice meditation, silence, and mindful walks. The more we silence external noise, the more clearly we hear the language of the universe.

It's important to remember that these signs don't always tell us what we want to hear. Sometimes they push us out of our comfort zones, to face uncomfortable truths, to change course. But they always do so from a place of loving wisdom. They're not there to manipulate us or scare us. They're there to awaken us, to guide us toward who we truly are. And when we follow them with humility, life becomes lighter, richer, more magical.

To live attentive to synchronicity is to live with an open heart. It's to recognize that we are part of an invisible fabric that connects everything. It's to realize that every moment can be a message, every encounter an opportunity, every difficulty a bridge to something greater. And the most beautiful thing is that we don't need to understand everything with our minds. We just need to trust, be grateful, and keep walking, knowing that the universe, in mysterious and perfect ways, is always speaking to us. It's just waiting for us to listen.

# Oneness with All That Is

There's an experience that many people seek throughout their lives, even if they don't always know how to put a name to it. It's a profound feeling of peace, of wholeness, of connection with all that exists. It's as if, for a moment, everything fits together, everything makes sense, and one can rest in an inner certainty that needs no words. This experience is the experience of oneness. It's not a philosophical idea or a complicated spiritual theory. It's a direct experience, a state of consciousness in which separation disappears and we feel that we are part of everything, and that everything is within us.

For most of our daily lives, we live under the illusion of separation. We believe we are isolated individuals, separate from other people, from nature, from the universe. We feel disconnected, as if everything is external, something that happens to us from outside. This way of seeing life is rooted in the ego, in the mind that classifies, judges, compares, and makes us constantly feel different and sometimes even in conflict with others. But deep within our being, there is a very different truth: we are not separate from anything. We are an expression of the same life, a spark from the same source. And when we begin to awaken to this truth, everything begins to change.

Unity doesn't mean the disappearance of our individuality. It's not about erasing our identity or making us all the same. Unity is a broader awareness, an understanding that, although each of us may have a different form, we all share the same essence. It's like the ocean and the waves: each wave is unique, but they are all water, all part of the same sea. Similarly, every person, every tree, every animal, every star is made of the same fundamental energy. Everything we see, touch, feel, and think is part of an invisible web of connection. Quantum physics already suggests this, and many spiritual traditions have affirmed it for centuries: there is no real separation between you and the universe.

Accessing this experience of unity is not something achieved intellectually. It's not enough to understand it as a pretty idea. Unity is lived. It is felt in the body, in the soul, in the heart. Sometimes it happens spontaneously, in moments of deep presence, in nature, in meditation, in an existential crisis. Other times, it is the result of a path of transformation, of much internal observation, of detachment, of silence. There is no single way to get there, but there are signs that tell us we are getting closer: we begin to judge less, to feel more compassion, to value the simple, to find beauty in the everyday, to live with more gratitude.

When a person experiences this unity, even for a few seconds, something within them transforms. They can no longer view life the same way. They can no longer treat others with indifference or cause harm without feeling that they are also hurting themselves. Because they realize, on a deep level, that what happens to others also happens to them. The boundary between "I" and "you" dissolves. A new sensitivity is born, a tenderness toward all that lives, a responsibility that arises not from duty, but from love. It's no longer about being good out of obligation, but about acting from the awareness that everything we do affects the whole, and that's why we choose more carefully, with more respect.

The experience of unity also changes our relationship with pain. We begin to see that our wounds are not merely personal, that we often carry pains that come from all of humanity, from our family history, from past generations. We understand that healing is not just an individual thing, but a contribution to the well-being of all. Likewise, joy is no longer a selfish experience. When we are happy from this awareness, that joy expands, spreads, illuminates. We become bridges of light, channels of harmony. Our very being is already medicine for the world.

Unity also helps us reconcile ourselves with death. When we believe we are only this body, this mind, this limited story, death seems like a threat, an end. But when we feel we are part of something eternal, death loses its weight. We know that the form transforms, but the essence remains. Life continues in other forms, in other cycles. Fear dissolves and gives way to a profound trust in mystery. We no longer need to control so much, nor fight against the natural flow of existence. We begin to live with more surrender, more serenity, more openness.

To live from unity is to live with humility. We no longer need to feel superior to anyone, because we understand that every being has its place and value. Even what seems dark, chaotic, or painful has a purpose in the fabric of life. It doesn't mean justifying suffering or injustice, but rather seeing beyond the apparent, with a gaze that includes and embraces. This vision isn't achieved overnight. It requires practice, patience, and, above all, honesty with oneself. But each step toward unity brings us closer to a fuller, truer, and more peaceful life.

One way to cultivate this awareness is through paying attention to the present moment. When we are fully present, without judgment, without distractions, we begin to feel that there is no separation between us and our surroundings. We merge with sound, with light, with silence. We can also nourish this experience by connecting with nature, with art, with breathing. Every act done with awareness is a gateway to unity. Every gesture of love is an affirmation that we are one.

And perhaps the most beautiful thing about all this is that unity isn't something we have to create. It's already here. It has always been. We are the ones who have forgotten, the ones who have disconnected. The work isn't to build something new, but to remember what we already are. It's a return, not a conquest. And in that return, we discover that there is nothing we lack, that everything we seek outside already lives within us. Because in the end, unity isn't out there. Unity begins when we look within and recognize that we have always been part of the whole, and that the whole lives within us.

# Valuing the Everyday from Consciousness

In daily life, we tend to move with so much haste, so much worry, so many plans and to-dos, that we often overlook the most essential things. We live waiting for grand and spectacular moments: a dream trip, an important achievement, a perfect relationship, a spiritual revelation. We were taught to seek distant goals, to dream of ideal futures, to pursue something that always seems to be further ahead. But meanwhile, the most valuable things are often right in front of us, in the everyday, in the simple, in the seemingly ordinary. Valuing the everyday from a conscious perspective is learning to see with new eyes what has always been there, and discovering that in every moment, if we are present, there is a profound richness waiting to be recognized.

Awareness is the key to transforming the ordinary into the extraordinary. When we are truly attentive, everything becomes more alive. The sound of falling water, the aroma of morning coffee, the sun shining through a window, a sincere conversation, the touch of the wind on our skin, a smile given to us unasked for. These are such simple moments that they might seem insignificant, but if we live them fully, they become true gifts. It's not about doing something special, but about being awake while living what we already do. It's not about changing our lives, it's about changing the way we live them.

Valuing the everyday isn't about settling. It's not about resigning yourself to a life without magic; on the contrary, it's about opening your eyes to the magic that's already present. It's about realizing that we don't need extraordinary things to feel fulfilled. Sometimes we think happiness lies in changing everything: our home, our job, our partner, our city. But then we discover that we can still feel empty even after these changes, because it's not the outside that gives meaning, but how we experience it. When we cultivate awareness, we begin to see that it doesn't matter so much where we are or what we're doing, but rather where we're doing it from. If we're present, everything comes alive.

One of the most common human mistakes is postponing gratitude. We think: when I have this, then I'll be happy. When I achieve that, then I'll be grateful. But gratitude isn't born from having, but from seeing. We can have little and feel fulfilled, or have much and feel empty. It all depends on whether or not we are connected to the present moment. And gratitude is a powerful form of connection. It's a way of honoring what we already have, of saying to life: I see you, I value you, I am grateful. Gratitude roots us in the present and opens our hearts. It makes us more sensitive, more humble, more human.

Many seek elevated spiritual experiences, higher states of consciousness, and that's fine. But we sometimes forget that spirituality isn't separate from daily life. It's not just found in temples, retreats, or sacred books. It's also found in washing dishes mindfully, listening wholeheartedly to a loved one, caring for a plant, walking leisurely, and preparing a meal with love. Every act can be sacred if we live it with presence. The everyday is the true arena of spiritual transformation. We don't need to escape our lives to grow; we just need to inhabit them with greater awareness.

This shift in perspective also allows us to discover beauty where we didn't see it before. We learn to enjoy silence, to find poetry in the routine, to connect with the natural rhythms of the day. Even tasks that once seemed boring or burdensome can become meditations if we pay attention to them. Sweeping can be a way to organize our minds. Cooking can be an act of love. Dressing calmly can be a moment of caring for our bodies. The key is to be truly present, to not do things out of habit, but with intention.

But it's not about forcing ourselves to enjoy everything. Life also has difficult moments, gray days, and uncomfortable emotions. Valuing everyday life with awareness also means embracing those moments. Not running away from them, not sugarcoating them, but living them with sincerity. Accepting discomfort when it comes, breathing in the midst of chaos, and supporting ourselves with compassion when we're sad. This attitude doesn't make us weak; on the contrary, it makes us more authentic and stronger. It helps us see that every emotion, every experience, has something to teach us. And that even in the midst of pain, there is beauty if we are present.

Furthermore, when we value the everyday, we also value the people around us more. We stop taking those who accompany us for granted. We realize how important a hug, a kind word, a look of understanding is. We stop seeking perfect relationships and begin to nurture the ones we already have, with patience, with love, with listening. Awareness makes us more attentive, more grateful, more available to others. It makes us see that each human being is a universe, and that sharing a sincere moment with someone is already a blessing.

Living this way doesn't mean everything will be easy or ideal. There will be days of tiredness, routine, and conflict. But if we're attentive, even those days teach us something. They remind us that life is a cycle, that there are times of expansion and stillness, of clarity and doubt. And that everything has its place. By living from awareness, we stop fighting life so much. We begin to flow with it, to cooperate with its rhythms, to trust its wisdom. And in that trust, we find peace.

Ultimately, valuing everyday life from a place of awareness is an act of love. Love for life as it is. Love for what is simple, for what is real, for what we have now. It means stopping looking outside for what is already within. It means stopping running and starting to be. And in doing so, we discover that we don't need more to be happy, that what we sought so far away was always here, in a cup of tea, in a true conversation, in a silent sunset. Life doesn't need to be perfect to be sacred. It just needs to be lived with an awakened heart.

# Conscious and Sacred Relationships

A conscious and sacred relationship is not an ideal fantasy or a relationship without conflict. It is not a perfect union where everything flows effortlessly and no one makes a mistake. On the contrary, it is a deeply human relationship, where both people commit to growing, knowing each other, supporting each other, and seeing the other not as an object to be fulfilled, but as a mirror and a companion on the journey. In this type of relationship, the goal is not to control or possess, but rather to understand, respect, and love more fully and freely. It is a relationship that nourishes the soul because it is built on authenticity, vulnerability, and presence.

The first thing that transforms a relationship into something conscious is intention. Being with someone to fill personal voids, to avoid loneliness, to meet social expectations, or to maintain a comfort zone isn't the same as being with someone with the sincere desire to share life's journey. A conscious relationship begins with the desire to truly know each other, without masks, without roles, without games. It's not about seeking in the other what one hasn't found within oneself, but rather about sharing from a more complete, more honest place. This doesn't mean we have to be perfect before being with someone, but rather that we are committed to our own process, that we have the willingness to look inward and take responsibility for our part in the relationship.

Love in a conscious relationship isn't limited to intense emotions, physical attraction, or romance. Those things may be present and welcome, but true love goes far beyond that. It's an act of will, a daily choice to be present, to care, to respect, even when there's disagreement or difficulty. A sacred relationship is based on deep communication, active listening, and mutual respect for each other's individual processes. The goal isn't always to be right, but rather to understand and be understood. Arguments aren't to win, but to build. Differences of opinion aren't seen as a threat, but as an opportunity to grow together.

A conscious relationship also involves acknowledging and embracing our wounds. We all bring into our relationships parts of ourselves that have been hurt, rejected, or ignored. In a superficial relationship, these wounds are hidden or projected onto the other. But in a conscious relationship, they are given space. It is recognized that the other is not here to heal our wounds, but can accompany us in the process. In this context, conflicts cease to be something to be avoided at all costs and become sacred moments, because they reveal what still needs attention, love, and understanding. The important thing is not never to argue, but how we do it and what we do with what is awakened within us.

Furthermore, in a conscious relationship, the other's freedom is deeply respected. It's not about merging into a single identity, nor expecting the other to renounce their essence to make us feel safe. Each person maintains their individual path, their passions, their time, their space. A union is built that doesn't imprison, but rather empowers. It is understood that the other is not here to complete us, but to share. From this understanding, jealousy, possessiveness, and excessive demands begin to lose their strength, because we realize that true love is not born from the fear of losing, but from the freedom to choose one another every day.

There is also a spiritual dimension to sacred relationships. Not necessarily because both people share the same practice or belief, but because they recognize each other as souls, not just bodies or personalities. There is a sense that something greater is guiding the encounter. Sometimes, there is even the feeling that this person has come to teach us something important, to accompany us on a stretch of the path, to help us remember who we are. This perception gives the relationship a different depth. Every experience together, from the most beautiful to the most painful, becomes part of a broader process of evolution.

Presence is another fundamental key. Many relationships are weakened by a lack of presence. Being physically with someone isn't the same as actually being there. A conscious relationship requires attention, quality time, and real connection. It's not about quantity, but about the intensity of the shared moment. A genuine look, a sincere conversation, a tender gesture can have more power than a thousand soulless routines. Presence means putting your phone aside, stopping thinking about what's next, and simply being with the other person—available, receptive, open.

Caring for others isn't imposed; it's born of true love. In a conscious relationship, caring for each other doesn't mean sacrificing or losing oneself, but rather being attentive to the other's well-being without neglecting one's own. There's a balance between giving and receiving, between accompanying and respecting boundaries. Empathy is practiced, and genuine interest is asked about how the other is doing, what they need, how they feel. And we learn to ask for what we need without manipulating, blaming, or demanding.

It's important to mention that a conscious relationship isn't a permanent or automatic state. It's a constant process. There are days of clarity and others of confusion. There are moments of deep connection and moments of distance. What's important is the mutual commitment to return again and again to the center, to choose love over ego, to learn from every experience together. Sometimes, the most loving act in a sacred relationship is knowing when to let go, when to let go without resentment, recognizing that each bond has its time and purpose.

Ultimately, a conscious and sacred relationship transforms us because it invites us to be our best selves, not out of obligation, but out of inspiration. It reflects our shadows and also our light. It shows us our resistances and also our potential. It helps us grow, heal, and love more deeply. And when two people meet from that place, they not only accompany each other, but also elevate each other. They become soul allies, companions in evolution, journeyers who, amidst their imperfect humanity, decide to love one another with awareness, with respect, and with the humility of those who know that true love is not possessed, it is cultivated.

# Life Purpose and Soul Vocation

Many people spend much of their lives feeling like something's missing, even though they seemingly have everything. They may have a stable job, a family, a sufficient income, even moments of fun, but deep inside they feel an emptiness they don't know how to fill. This feeling, often confusing and silent, is often a sign that they're not connected to their true life purpose, to what they really came here to do. It's not just about having a job or achieving external goals, but about aligning with something deeper, something that comes from the soul. Discovering and living one's life purpose isn't a luxury for a select few; it's a vital necessity for anyone who wants to live a full, meaningful, and authentic life.

Life purpose is not an externally imposed obligation, nor an idea that must follow other people's trends or expectations. It's not about having a fancy title or achieving fame or recognition. Life purpose is rather an inner direction, an impulse that comes from the heart, an energy that moves us with natural enthusiasm when we are doing what truly corresponds to us. It is what fills us with life, what makes us lose track of time, what awakens our creativity and connects us with others through service and love. It is not something invented; it is something discovered, something that has always been within us, but which requires attention, silence, and honesty to manifest.

The soul's vocation is the way in which that purpose takes shape in the world. It is the concrete way in which we decide to embody that inner calling. It can be through art, medicine, teaching, spiritual guidance, the simplest of jobs, or social projects. No vocation is more important than another, because all are distinct expressions of the same impulse to live meaningfully. What matters is not what we do, but where we do it from. When what we do is aligned with who we are deepest, life flows more clearly, even in the midst of challenges.

Discovering your soul's calling requires courage, because it often goes against what others expect of us. Perhaps we grew up believing we should follow a safe, profitable, or family-approved path, but over time we feel that this shuts us down, disconnects us. Listening to your soul may involve changing course, letting go of old ideas, or going through moments of uncertainty. But each step in that direction brings with it renewed energy, a sense of being truly alive. The soul doesn't shout, it whispers. And if we don't listen to those whispers in time, life often shocks us into paying attention.

To connect with our life purpose, we need to get in touch with ourselves. There are no exact formulas or one-size-fits-all paths, but there are common signs that can guide us. One of them is joy. What genuinely brings us joy, what makes us feel light and excited, is often related to our purpose. Another sign is natural ability. There are things we do well without much effort, talents we've had since childhood, activities we could do for hours without tiring. There's also the call of the heart, that voice that tells us there's something more, even if we don't quite know what it is. That persistent feeling that we've come here for something special, even though the world tells us to settle for what's safe.

Purpose isn't always revealed all at once; sometimes we discover it piecemeal, as if we were putting together a puzzle. Perhaps we start by doing something small that fulfills us, and that leads us to new opportunities, new people, new understandings. The important thing is to move, to act, to try. The soul needs movement to express itself. Paralysis due to fear or perfectionism only delays the process. It doesn't matter if we don't have complete clarity at first; the important thing is to take the next step with sincerity and trust that the path will open up.

It's also essential to understand that purpose isn't fixed. It's not one thing that lasts a lifetime. We can have various forms of expression; we can change, evolve, adapt. What remains is the internal energy, the deep intention. What changes is the way we express it according to the stages of life, according to what reality demands of us. Sometimes our purpose is to care for someone, another time to create a work, and later to teach or heal. All can be part of the same purpose if we do it from the soul.

Another important point is that life's purpose isn't always lived out in grand settings. It's often found in the small, the everyday, the seemingly simple. A loving gesture, a wise word, a compassionate attitude can be pure expressions of our calling. We don't have to wait for grand conditions to live with purpose. We can start now, where we are, with what we have. Life doesn't demand perfection, it demands authenticity. Every moment is an opportunity to act with meaning, to put soul into what we do.

Living aligned with purpose transforms us profoundly. We feel more fulfilled, more centered, more connected to life. Fatigue changes its flavor, because even when there is effort, there is also satisfaction. Fear still exists, but it no longer paralyzes, because there is something stronger that sustains it. Even pain becomes different, because when we know we are on the right path, any challenge is experienced as part of a growth process. Life ceases to be a series of tasks to accomplish and becomes a meaningful dance.

Therefore, it's essential to pause in our lives to ask ourselves: Am I living in a way that is consistent with who I am? Does what I do connect me with my soul or distance me from it? What activities energize me? What would I like to do even if I weren't paid? What legacy do I want to leave, beyond the material? These questions aren't answered with the mind, but with experience, with silence, with the heart. It's not about looking outside for the perfect answer, but about going within and learning to listen.

Life purpose and soul calling aren't imposed, they're remembered. We all have a compass within us that knows where to go. We just need to learn to listen to it, trust it, and have the courage to follow it. When we live from this perspective, we not only transform ourselves, but we also inspire others. We become living lights that illuminate the path, not because we want to be admired, but because we are being what we came to be. And there is no greater joy than that.

# Service as an Expression of Higher Consciousness

In a world where we are often taught to compete, hoard, and protect our own, the concept of service may seem strange or even weak. But when we speak of service from a higher consciousness, we are not referring to sacrificing ourselves out of obligation or being submissive. We are referring to a way of living in which we understand that we are not separate from others, that what happens to them also affects us, that true well-being is collective, not individual. Service, understood from this profound perspective, is a natural expression of an awakened soul, one that has understood its connection to all that exists and that has decided to contribute to the world from a place of love, compassion, and wisdom.

Serving doesn't mean losing oneself in others or forgetting oneself. Nor is it about pleasing everyone or living according to what others need. True service is born from plenitude, not from lack. When a person has worked on themselves, healed wounds, integrated their shadow, and found meaning in their life, they naturally begin to look outward from a different perspective. They no longer act out of fear, approval, or duty, but out of free choice. They want to help because they know their well-being is linked to the well-being of the whole. Service then becomes an authentic expression of the love that dwells within them.

A higher consciousness isn't content to simply look at its own achievements. It seeks to transcend the ego and put personal gifts at the service of the common good. And the most beautiful thing is that this kind of service doesn't have to be spectacular or public. It can manifest itself in very simple and silent gestures. Listening attentively to someone who is suffering, tenderly accompanying a sick person, preparing a meal with love, caring for a plant or an animal with respect, teaching from the heart, working with honesty and joy—all of these are also service. You don't have to travel to another country or found a large organization to serve. You can begin where you are, with what you have.

Intention is what makes the difference. Even things done out of routine or interest can be transformed into sacred acts if done with awareness. That's why it's important to ask ourselves: Where am I acting from? Is what I do connected to my heart or just my fears? When we pay attention to these questions, we realize that any action can be a form of service if it's guided by presence, humility, and a genuine desire to contribute to the well-being of others. It's not about being perfect, but about being awake and available.

Serving also transforms the one serving. It's not a path of simple renunciation, but of profound growth. When we give from the soul, something within us expands. We feel useful, alive, connected. Our ego deflates a little, and we stop taking ourselves so seriously. We learn to look at others with more empathy, to value the diversity of experiences, and to let go of judgments. We discover that helping doesn't mean having all the answers, but rather being present and open. Sometimes the most transformative thing isn't what we say or do, but how we look, how we touch, how we carry ourselves.

Conscious service also protects us from spiritual narcissism, from the temptation to believe we're more advanced than others because we've read certain books, practiced certain techniques, or achieved certain states. True spiritual advancement is measured by the capacity to love, to share, to build community. A truly awakened person doesn't lock themselves away in their tower of light, but rather goes out into the world, gets their hands dirty, and gets involved. They know they didn't come just to be enlightened, but to be a channel of light for others.

Furthermore, service helps heal many personal wounds. It frees us from mental isolation, self-pity, and drama. When we focus on alleviating the suffering of others, our own pain is transformed. This doesn't mean we should ignore what we feel, but sometimes, by stopping revolving around ourselves, we find a strength we didn't know we had. Serving makes us resilient; it connects us to something greater than our individual history. It's as if the soul remembers its true nature through every act of giving.

Service can also be a form of creative expression. Some people serve by writing, others by cooking, others by designing harmonious spaces, others by caring for animals, others by creating community projects. There is no single path. The important thing is that each person discovers their own way of contributing, their unique way of being useful, without copying others' models. What inspires you, what ignites you, may be just what the world needs. Don't underestimate the value of what you can offer. Often, one word from you can change someone's day, or their life. And you don't even know it.

When we understand service as an expression of higher consciousness, we also learn to do so within healthy boundaries. It's not about exhausting oneself or saving everyone. One serves from what one can, without losing oneself, without forcing oneself, without expecting rewards. It's a free, fluid giving that also respects rest, silence, and the need to nourish oneself. One cannot serve from a vacuum, which is why it's so important to first inhabit, know, and care for oneself. Service is not opposed to self-love; it includes it. A person who loves and respects themselves serves better.

And finally, serving from a place of conscience is also a revolutionary act. In a world that often prioritizes self-interest, appearances, and speed, a person who acts from compassion and conscience is sowing a different seed. They may not change the entire world immediately, but they do transform their surroundings, inspire others, and create small networks of light that expand. Every gesture counts. Every loving act creates a new field. Every time we choose to serve, we are saying yes to a more awakened, more just, and more humane humanity.

Service as an expression of higher consciousness is not a task, it's a way of being.

A way that emerges naturally when we understand who we really are and why we are here. It is the living manifestation of the soul that has found itself and, therefore, can do nothing but share. Because once one has tasted the fullness of living awake, one cannot turn back. One wants to give, simply because love needs to move. And true service is that: love in motion.

# Towards a Conscious Humanity

Imagine a world in which every human being walks through life with their eyes open—not just their physical eyes, but also those of their heart, those of their conscience. A world where every gesture, every word, and every decision is made from a deep place of understanding, respect, and love. That is the vision of a conscious humanity. It is not an impossible utopia; it is a real possibility that begins within each of us. Because conscious humanity is not something imposed from the outside, but something that is built from within, from millions of individuals who choose to live awake.

A conscious humanity is not defined solely by technological advances, scientific discoveries, or economic achievements. It is defined by the quality of its presence, by its capacity to see the other as a mirror, by its ability to act with compassion, by its willingness to heal collective wounds. It is a humanity that no longer needs to divide between "us" and "them," between "good" and "bad," but rather recognizes the fundamental unity of all that exists. It understands that the pain of one is the pain of all and that the joy of one can uplift many.

This shift toward a conscious humanity requires a new kind of leadership, not based on external power, but on internal power. People who lead by example, who embody the values they preach, who listen more than they speak, who are driven not by ego but by inner wisdom. But it also requires awakened communities, families that educate with love and not fear, schools that teach how to think and not just memorize, and media that report truth and not sensationalism.

It is a profound, systemic, but above all, human change.

One of the pillars of this transformation is individual responsibility. We cannot wait for the world to change if we continue to react out of fear, anger, and indifference. Every person who dares to look within themselves, to recognize their shadows, to heal their wounds, to transform their pain into wisdom, is contributing to this collective change. It's not easy work, but it is essential. Because only when we stop blaming others and take responsibility for our part, do we begin to move toward a different way of living—freer, more authentic, more luminous.

Consciousness also implies presence. A conscious humanity doesn't run aimlessly, doesn't act out of inertia, or live on autopilot. It learns to stop, to listen, to feel. It reconnects with the earth, with its body, with nature, with the present moment. A society that honors the here and now is one that doesn't get lost in the past or obsess over the future. It lives every moment as a gift, as an opportunity to grow, to love, to learn.

On this path toward a conscious humanity, it is also essential to heal our relationship with the earth. We can no longer act as if we were the owners of nature. We are part of it, not its masters. An awakened humanity recognizes that the planet is not a resource; it is a living being that sustains us and deserves to be cared for. This change is not just about recycling or planting trees; it is about a change of perspective, about once again experiencing the sacredness of life in all its forms, about acting from a place of gratitude rather than exploitation.

Another essential aspect is emotional awakening. For centuries, we were taught to repress what we felt, to view emotions as weaknesses. But a conscious humanity understands that emotions are part of intelligence, that feeling is also knowing. Learning to manage what we feel, to express it without hurting, to understand what lies behind each emotion, is key to building healthy relationships, peaceful environments, and more just societies. Spiritual growth is not just a matter of the mind or meditation; it also involves the heart.

Education plays a central role in this collective awakening. It's not enough to teach content; we must educate for life, for the soul. A conscious education develops complete human beings, not just professionals. It teaches us to think critically, to connect with intuition, to resolve conflicts with empathy, to value diversity, to question what seems normal if that normality is harmful. When we educate from love and freedom, we are raising generations who will not repeat the mistakes of the past, but will dare to create something new.

A conscious humanity also transforms the way we relate. We no longer seek others to fill voids, to control, or to possess. We seek them to share, to grow together, to learn. Conscious relationships are based on honesty, authenticity, and mutual respect. They are understood as sacred spaces where two souls meet, not to complete each other, but to accompany one another. This way of connecting not only improves relationships, it also changes how we relate at work, in the family, and in society.

Art and creativity also flourish in an awakened humanity. When people live from consciousness, their expression becomes deeper, more beautiful, more connected to the essential. Art ceases to be mere entertainment and becomes medicine for the soul, a vehicle for transformation. Words, colors, shapes, music—everything becomes the language of the spirit. And this inspires, uplifts, and heals. Because in a world often plagued by superficiality, conscious art reminds us of who we are in essence.

And finally, a conscious humanity does not forget the soul. Beyond the body, the mind, the emotions, there is something within us that does not die, that does not change, that silently observes, that knows. Connecting with that eternal part is the deepest step of awakening. No matter what you call it, the important thing is that you recognize it and listen to it. A society that honors the soul is a society that lives with meaning, with purpose, with direction. It does not allow itself to be dragged down by confusion or despair, because it knows there is an inner compass that guides, even in the darkness.

Moving toward a conscious humanity is the most urgent and most beautiful journey of our time. There are no magic formulas or shortcuts. It is a path taken step by step, moment by moment, person by person. But it is a possible path. And it is already underway. More and more people are awakening, looking inward, choosing to live from love and not from fear. That is the true revolution. Silent, profound, luminous. A revolution that does not destroy, but transforms. And you are part of it.

www.ingramcontent.com/pod-product-compliance
Lightning Source LLC
LaVergne TN
LVHW090417210926
848480LV00002B/603